More Praise for
Planner Pet Peeves

"Someone finally has the courage to tell suppliers the truth about what planners think. In an industry that relies on collaboration, *Planner Pet Peeves* provides valuable insight that is guaranteed to improve communication and understanding between suppliers and planners. It's a must-read book for anyone who wants to provide more effective event solutions for their customers."
– *Michael Vennerstrom, President, Equinox Creative*

"This is an eye-opener into the heads of professional meeting planners and how they make buying decisions. Through reading this book and absorbing the content, suppliers will learn to communicate better, build relationships, and SELL."
– *Julie Giorgio, Bloomington, Minnesota CVB*

"Shawna's book is an eye-opener for all in the meetings industry. 'People Buy People First' is never more true than now. The power of personal endorsement remains the most influential way to develop business today."
– *Derek Wallace, Owner, Wallace Travel Group, Ireland*

Planner Pet Peeves

Straight Talk for Suppliers to
Understand How Planners
Really Think, Act and Buy

Shawna Suckow, CMP

© 2012 Shawna Suckow

All Rights Reserved

ISBN-13: 978-1470098681

Printed in the United States of America

First Edition

Dedication

to my family

Table of Contents

Section I: Brace Yourself... 9

Section II: Building Relationships 19

1. How's That Fax Machine Working...
2. Telephone Dos and Don'ts
3. eCommunications
4. Snail Mail
5. Networking
6. Tradeshows & Hosted Buyer Events
7. Sponsorships
8. Advertising
9. Apparently I Struck a Nerve

Section III: Hotels 77

10. The Dreaded RFP Process
11. Site Inspections
12. Contracts
13. Fees, Fees, Ridiculous Fees
14. CSMs
15. Food & Beverage

Section IV: Non-Hotel Suppliers 121

16. Convention & Visitor Bureaus
17. Destination Management Companies
18. Convention Centers
19. Transportation Companies

Section V: Starting Now 147

SECTION I.

Brace Yourself...

"Ch-ch-ch-ch-changes
(turn and face the strain)"
–from the David Bowie song *Changes*

Planner Pet Peeves

Section I: Brace Yourself...

This is not Going to be Easy to Hear...

Times are a-changin', but you already knew that. What you are doing is not working the same way it used to. In the meetings and events industry, we don't buy the same way we used to buy, and we don't communicate the same way we did before. Do you still sell the same way? The economy has changed, our industry continues to evolve, and technology continues to transform everything. To those who think the way they have always sold is still fine—this is your wake-up call.

In today's over-communicated, media-glutted world, we need to relearn how to talk and connect and do business with one another. This means suppliers have to approach sales in

Planner Pet Peeves

an entirely different way, or we planners won't respond.

More than ever before, buyers are expecting to build relationships, not just make a purchase and move on.

"I wish all vendors approached our working relationship as a partnership," said Daphne Meyers, CMM, Events Marketing Specialist with AE2S out of North Dakota. "I am there to work with them and meet their business needs, and I want the same in return."

Yet while we expect these partnerships with our suppliers, we've made it harder than ever for you to form them with us. We are so busy keeping our heads down and getting through the day's workload that we have cocooned ourselves away from the distraction of interaction. It is rare these days for us to actually pick up a phone call, respond to an email, or make time for an industry event.

In order to cut through all the clutter and noise in our day and get our attention, suppliers have to be willing to try new sales tactics because the same-old-same-old will not do. Do you ever feel, as a supplier, that you're just spinning your wheels these days? That is because in all likelihood, you are. So how do you fix it?

In researching this book, I heard the same recurring pet peeves from planner after planner across North America. We have definite preferences for how we want to do business with suppliers, yet we never share those with you.

If you could read our minds, you would learn how to build the perfect relationship, and how to sell to us in the way we want to be sold.

Wouldn't that be a game changer? Wouldn't that make your job so much easier? I think it would make the planner's job a lot easier, too.

I wrote this book to eliminate this huge black hole of communication between our two camps: the suppliers and the planners. Industry change comes from small actions that cause ripple effects, which in turn become new norms once there is enough buy-in. So if this book results in some small actions that ultimately result in better communications between planners and suppliers, then I have accomplished my goal.

To Suppliers Everywhere:

You may think this book is entirely one-sided, and admittedly, you're right.

To write this book, I gathered information and opinions solely from planners, not suppliers. Why? Because suppliers hold the power to lead the change, and in return, you'll reap huge benefits. You just need to understand how we planners *really* think, and how we make our buying decisions.

No supplier wants to unwittingly do or say something that results in lost business without being given a fair shake.

If suppliers could just get into our planner brains and figure out how our strange breed thinks and acts...

Well, hold onto your seat. In the pages that follow, you'll get the rare opportunity to be a fly on the wall, hearing exactly what planners think, and what you can do to create stronger relationships.

Researching & Gathering this Information

In my role as president of SPIN, I've been given a wonderful opportunity to spend the last few years observing, researching, and interviewing senior-level planners of all kinds, from all over North America in round tables, panels, webinars and seminars. I've asked tough questions and requested pure honesty, however uncomfortable.

They candidly told me—planner-to-planner — what many of them have spent decades keeping from you, the industry suppliers.

I know that is frustrating to hear, but consider who we are. Planners are people-pleasers by nature. We don't burn bridges; we just walk downstream and find a new bridge. If we're unhappy with a supplier, many times they simply just never hear from us again. Unprofessional? We don't see it that way. Many of us believe that constant griping isn't the way to behave, and probably will do everyone more harm than good, so why bother? There are plenty of other suppliers out there, so we just go find one that's a better fit.

Planner Pet Peeves

That's why it was imperative for me to provide information that was painfully honest and no-holds-barred (otherwise, what's the point?). I hope that what I share in this book will change how suppliers communicate, build relationships, and sell.

Suppliers who have all this insider information undoubtedly will outperform the competition when it comes to building profitable and lasting relationships. As countless planners have told me, where there's a strong relationship, they're typically loyal to the *salesperson*, not the property or company. So your strongest relationships will follow you throughout your career.

Bear with me, because this information is extremely candid and not for thin-skinned folk. In order for change to happen, there needs to be perfect honesty, with no sugar-coating.

I promise it will be worth it. You will be more successful dealing with us once you understand us.

Section I: Brace Yourself...

You Should Know...

The information gathered and presented in this book is strictly from senior-level planners, and may not reflect the opinions of other generations of planners. Also, although I've spent a great deal of time listening to my peers and recording their thoughts in this book, I don't purport to speak for all my peers. There are always exceptions, and there are planners who certainly will disagree with what I'm about to share.

Planner Pet Peeves

SECTION II.

Building Relationships

"Excellence is to do a common thing in an uncommon way." - Booker T. Washington

Planner Pet Peeves

CHAPTER 1.

How's That Fax Machine Working For You?

Most senior-level planners (defined by SPIN, the Senior Planners Industry Network, as having more than 10 years of experience) will admit readily that it is nearly impossible to get in touch with us. By and large, we do not answer the phone anymore, we do not return every voice mail message, we do not respond to every single email, and we do not attend a lot of industry networking events these days. Yet, senior-level planners typically control the largest pieces of business, the largest number of annual events, and manage the largest teams in the industry. So who do you think suppliers are calling on the most, with the least results? Us.

So what's a supplier to do? Well, I can tell you with 100% certainty that what worked in the 1990s and 2000s no longer works today.

It's not a numbers game anymore – you can't do 'shotgun sales' and hope to hit something.

The advent of the Internet and social media has leveled the playing field – every supplier has access to the same huge virtual database of prospects. It's how you engage with those prospects that will make all the difference going forward. That's getting more and more challenging, though.

You can blame your slowing sales on the economy, but it's more than that. I believe time will tell—when the economy recovers, yes your business might improve. When the tide comes in, all boats rise. In this case, though, I strongly believe that if you're not adapting to the changing industry, you will lose out to the competition in the long run.

Remember fax machines? Wow, those were amazing contraptions when they first appeared in our offices. Fewer mailed packages, quicker response times to contracts, the benefits were quite clear. Today, if your fax machine collects anything but dust, technology is leaving you behind.

How great was email when it came around? Wow – it was amazing, a wonderful tool that saved us countless hours on the phone tracking people down. Today, you're lucky if you can get us to read what you send us, and getting a reply is even more challenging. Did you know that several years ago, many major universities stopped assigning email addresses to incoming freshmen? It's because the next generation sees email as *obsolete*. A friend's twenty-something niece told her that *email is for old people*.

What's my point, you ask? Every tool you use to connect with planners eventually becomes obsolete, and replaced by a better, more sure-fire method. It's happening right now. If you're not seeking out new sales methods and new ways of building relationships, you'll become obsolete along with email in the next decade.

Planner Pet Peeves

Section II: Building Relationships

CHAPTER 2.

Telephone Dos and Don'ts

Following the economic downturn and subsequent slow recovery, we've all been doing more with less.   Planners are keeping their heads down, often doing the added workload of their laid-off colleagues, and just trying to make it through day-by-day. Meanwhile, supplier marketing budgets have been cut, business is suffering, and the typical Director of Sales has told her team to double up on the cold-calling. It's a perfect storm: you're redoubling your cold calling efforts, and we're redoubling our efforts to avoid you.

Planner Pet Peeves

> **COLD CALLING** [kohld **kaw**-ling] *n.*
>
> 1. An activity known to be a complete waste of time. 2. An archaic technique preferred by salespeople of the previous century, with dubious results. Antonym: *see WARM CALLING*

Let me be perfectly clear on this: <u>your cold calls are our number one pet peeve</u>. Period. If we pick up the phone at all, we immediately are irritated and defensive before you even utter a word. This is no way to start off on the right foot. It's a losing battle that you magically have to try to turn around in the first 10 seconds of your call, which is nearly impossible against such odds. In other words, it is a complete waste of your time, and ours. You hang up, happy that you made a new connection. We hang up and curse ourselves for answering an unknown number, and remind ourselves not to do that again.

Planners overwhelmingly tell me the number one thing they hate when they get a cold call is that the supplier has done absolutely no prior research. The supplier uses that time to begin the conversation from square one: "So, can you tell me what type of meetings you plan, and where you plan them?"

It's amazing to me how many calls like this that I get out of the blue, from cities, hotels and various suppliers, and I'm not even remotely a viable lead for 99.9% of them. It usually goes like this: "Hi Shawna, this is Jane Doe from Anytown, USA. Just touching base with you today to see if you ever book meetings in our part of the country."

Clearly this poor supplier has a call quota to reach, and is quite obviously working a list, or shooting in the dark with no qualifying data. What a waste of her time and mine.

"When they mispronounce my name (which they almost all do), that's my number one pet peeve," said Sharon Schenk, CMP, Founder, Your Meeting Professional out of Connecticut. "Number two is them not knowing who I am. Look me up on LinkedIn. Google me. Find out where I've been and what I've done before you call me and try to sell me something. Everyone's trying to do their job, I get it, but do a little homework first."

The volume of this type of call increased exponentially when the economy took a downturn. Is it any wonder that many (if not most) planners don't pick up the phone anymore unless they recognize the number?

| Planner Pet Peeves

"The calls that I've been getting have been from hotels from which I have requested an RFP in the past," said Linda Hurtley, Meeting Planner, The Linwood Group out of Minneapolis. "I haven't contacted them, and they haven't contacted me, sometimes in five years, and now they're calling me. I ask them to take me off their list."

I believe that cold calls these days aren't about building relationships at all; they're about meeting quotas and keeping your boss happy - am I right? That's why I hope your boss reads this too, because we need to change and evolve away from this.

Warm Calling

So your boss is cracking the whip to double your cold calling efforts, thinking this is a grand idea. Budgets are cut, and calls are cheap, so this is how they figure you can catch the low hanging fruit out there: the rare planner waiting by the phone, pining for your call so she can buy exactly what you're selling. Riiiiiight.

If you absolutely have to call us, there are some tools out there to help you turn cold calls into warm calls. The best out there currently is

LinkedIn. With just one quick step, you can go from zero to much better results. A quick look at our profiles will tell you a lot of things that will enable that first call to go much smoother, and we'll be more receptive.

We share on LinkedIn where we've worked, often the type of meetings we've planned, and sometimes even the budgets we've controlled. We list awards we've won, associations we belong to, places we volunteer, hobbies we enjoy, and even books we've read.

During your first phone call to us, mention if we have something in common: where we went to school, where we might have crossed paths previously in this tight-knit industry, places we've lived. Mention if we know the same person, and (presuming we like and respect that mutual connection), you're in a good position to continue the conversation. It humanizes you to us, and softens our defenses right away. You're no longer an annoyance who's out to waste our time; you're an industry colleague with something in common.

Planner Pet Peeves

> **A Better First Call**
>
> Supplier: "Hi Shawna, this is Steve from XYZ Computer Rental."
>
> Me: <Sigh> "Hi Steve."
>
> Supplier: "I don't want to take up more than a minute of your time. I just wanted to let you know that I visited your LinkedIn profile, and we both know Claire Jones."
>
> Me: "Oh yes, Claire's a great friend – we serve on a committee together."
>
> Supplier: "I've done lots of business with her and I would like to be on your radar, too. Can I email you some information?"
>
> Me: "Absolutely – I look forward to it."
>
> Supplier: "Great – I'll get it to you today. Say hi to Claire for me next time you see her."
>
> Note: Next time I speak with Claire, I will probably recall this mutual connection and ask her about him. One good word from a trusted industry colleague goes miles further than anything your marketing materials could ever say about you. Plus it turned your call from a bother to a pleasure.

In the next section, I'll show you how to do deep searches on LinkedIn.

What about Voice Mail?

Assuming you end up in voice mail most of the time when you are cold calling, what's the best way to get us to respond? I've heard many planners suggest that you leave your email address and phone number, so we can respond how we prefer. I myself am much more likely to respond via email, so those who give me this option are more likely to hear back. Others suggest that you keep your message low-key: just a brief overview, a mention of something we have in common or some research you've done about us or our meetings. Don't leave every detail about your property in our voice mail.

Tell us you want to be respectful of our time, and that you'd like to set up a five-minute appointment that fits our schedule. Tell us we don't have to call you back, that you'll follow up with us down the road (believe me, this is a relief and scores you points - we don't have time to return every message when many aren't relevant to our immediate needs).

Planner Pet Peeves

Ditch the Cold Calls for a Month!

If your boss is old-school and insists on cold calling, see if you can strike a deal for one month: switch your contact method to LinkedIn and track your success compared to the previous month. I guarantee it will be far more impressive and garner far more responses than cold calling. I'll show you how we planners prefer it to be done in the next section.

Section II: Building Relationships

CHAPTER 3.

eCommunications

eMail vs. LinkedIn

Planners all across North America have been very clear on their preferred forms of communication. Who answers every supplier phone call that comes in? Nobody. Who responds to every supplier email that comes in? (Maybe a handful of planners with too much time on their hands, or a guilt complex.) Who reads every LinkedIn invitation or message they receive? <u>Close to 100%!</u> (I find that those who don't are typically not on

LinkedIn due to corporate policy or personal preference).

"I like LinkedIn," said Linda Hurtley, Meeting Planner, The Linwood Group in Minneapolis. "I do read every invitation." Planners across North America say the same thing.

Will it last? Like email, the novelty eventually will wear off, and it will become somewhat of a nuisance, but for the next few years, there is an amazing window of opportunity for suppliers using LinkedIn. While this window of opportunity lasts, it is by far the most preferred method of initial communication according to most senior-level planners. So using LinkedIn to initially connect with planners is overwhelmingly better received than any other current form of communication.

How to Find the *Right* Planners on LinkedIn

Did you know you can do advanced searches on LinkedIn to identify planners in different industries, in specific zip codes, or even by title or company type? You also can do a company search and LinkedIn tells you which existing connections of yours are connected to someone at that company. LinkedIn even allows you to save these searches, and notifies you when there are new planners added to each search category.

How to Perform an Industry Search on LinkedIn

Say your target market includes government and pharmaceutical planners all across the U.S. That is a huge market segment to identify. LinkedIn offers a great way to search for planners by industry.

1. Log into LinkedIn
2. In the far upper right of the page under your name, you will see a search field, a blue magnifying glass icon, and then the word "Advanced." Click it.
3. You are now on the Advanced People Search page. A bit down the page you'll see the "Industries" box. Scroll down and check the boxes next to your desired industries.
4. Below the "Industries" box, you will see a "Relationship" box. I usually check 1st Level and Group connections only, because those are the folks I can immediately connect with – 2nd and 3rd level are more time-consuming.

Planner Pet Peeves

5. TIP: LinkedIn lets you belong to 50 groups. I recommend you join 50 groups where your target market hangs out. Search for groups by keyword like MPI, EventPeeps, BizBash, or more generic words like events, meetings, etc. This way, when you search for Group connections, your field of potential leads will be dramatically increased.

6. To narrow down your list, you can enter a zip code in the top section of this page, or a title. I find lots of planners by entering in an industry designation like CMP, CMM, CSAE, etc. in the keyword field.

7. TIP: Looking just for Association planners? Put the word "Association" in the company field. Looking just for corporate planners? Put the word "Corporation" or "Corp." or "Inc." into the company field. If you upgrade to a paid LinkedIn membership, you can even isolate your searches to just Fortune 1000 companies.

What if you are planning a sales trip to a new city and have only a handful of contacts? You can find potential contacts via a zip code search.

Finding Planners by Geographic Area on LinkedIn

1. In the far upper right of the LinkedIn Home page under your name, you will see a search field, a blue magnifying glass icon, and then the word "Advanced." Click it.

2. You are now on the Advanced People Search page. In the Zip Code field, enter any zip code in the city you'll be visiting, and select what radius you want to search, whether 10, 25, 50 miles, etc.

3. Enter in a Keyword to limit your search to planners, such as CMP, CMM, MPI, CAE, etc.

4. Important: scroll down to the "Relationships" box before you hit enter. Check the boxes for 1st Level and Group only; you can't connect with 2nd or 3rd level connections without a hassle, so keep it simple.

Want to Find Who the Planners are at a Specific Company?

A few years ago, I was planning a large expo geared toward men. It was taking place in

Planner Pet Peeves

Minneapolis, home to Buffalo Wild Wings. In my opinion, this was a sponsorship match made in heaven, if I could just get my foot in the door and make the right connection. I tried cold calling, left a couple messages, and never got a response. I asked around to see if any of my colleagues knew anyone at BWW. I emailed my extended circle, still no connection.

Then it dawned on me to do a company search in LinkedIn. I discovered that my former employee was a first-level connection with their marketing director! Turns out they were roommates in college. One simple call to my former employee and I got the introduction, and got the meeting. Had I started with LinkedIn in the first place, I would have saved myself a lot of wasted time.

> **How to Perform a Specific Company Search in LinkedIn**
>
> 1. From the LinkedIn Home page, click on "Companies" in the bar at the top of the page.
> 2. On the "Companies" page, enter the company name.

> 3. You will see a list of any contacts within that company with whom you have a direct or indirect connection. Voila.

If you want to dig deeper, a simple Google search of a planner's name will tell you at least some of the cities where we've held meetings or events in recent years. Google my name - I come up as a contact for one meeting or another, such as SPINCon. If you then Google SPINCon 2012, you'll see where we've been. If you Google future years (i.e. "SPINCon 2014), you'll get a better idea of what destinations a planner has selected for future years (or better yet, find out that they have not placed our meeting for a particular year, and you have uncovered an opportunity).

This may take you a few extra minutes for each planner you want to call, but 10 effective calls per day sure beats 30 dead-end calls. I guarantee that you will be far more successful and well-received, instead of unknowingly starting off on the wrong foot like so many suppliers do when cold calling.

Planner Pet Peeves

> **About YOUR LinkedIn Profile...**
>
> Don't list all the sales records you've broken, or how you've consistently exceeded your quarterly or annual goals. We planners regularly check out your profiles too, before deciding to connect with you, return your call, etc. If you come across as a shark, how much do you think we'll trust you to be a fair and equitable business partner from the get-go? Not much.
>
> Humanize your profile, share charities you support, hobbies, books, anything we might have in common that will turn you from a salesperson into a potential business partner. It's a known fact that people do business with people they like, so give us reasons to like you, not distrust you.

How to Ensure a Planner Will Delete Your LinkedIn Invitation to Connect

Even though planners overwhelmingly prefer LinkedIn, they still have their preferences about how it's done. They almost unanimously hate when they receive generic requests to connect, especially if the person indicates they are a friend or colleague when they are not.

> **Did You Know?**
>
> Did you know that LinkedIn allows you to join up to fifty groups? I recommend joining groups where your target audience congregates. When you call, tell me that we're in the same group on LinkedIn and that you liked my recent comment on the discussion board (provided I've made one). You could even start your own discussion on LinkedIn, asking a candid question that planners are sure to respond to (how about posting "How do planners feel about cold calls these days?").

Before you send an invitation to connect, change that generic language: "I'd like to add you to my professional network on LinkedIn." Make it brief, personable and non-salesy. Tell the planner you just want to be on her radar for any future needs. Don't--I repeat don't--use this invitation as a sales pitch. It will fail and you're likely to be ignored. LinkedIn is a *social* network: picture it like a virtual cocktail reception for work. You wouldn't walk up to someone, hand them a brochure and walk away. You would make a little small talk, find something in common, humanize yourself, and *then* talk shop.

> ### A LinkedIn Success Story
>
> I tell this story every time I teach a webinar or seminar about LinkedIn or sales techniques. It's an excellent example of using LinkedIn in the perfect way, in my opinion. It was in 2010 and I was busy planning our very first Atlanta SPIN gathering (we call them SPIN Think Tanks). I was struggling to convince the senior-planner community there to give the event a try. This is nothing new - our members are typically the last to take time out of the office for themselves, especially for something brand new to the area.
>
> Right around that time, I got a LinkedIn invitation from a sales manager named Kevin Priger from the Atlanta Marriott Gwinnett Place. His message had great timing and was perfectly unobtrusive. He said that he had heard about our first Atlanta Think Tank coming up, and wished us well. He also offered to help me in any way he could. Period. No sales pitch about his property, no offer of a site tour while I was in town, no mention of a follow-up email with photos and floor plans.

> I immediately called Kevin and asked for his help spreading the word about our Think Tank to his senior-planner contacts in the area. He sent out a blast email, and registrations immediately increased. Because of his selfless offer to help, and specifically because he did not give me the standard initial sales pitch, he stood out as someone truly interested in building a relationship, not making a quota. I now consider him one of authentic trusted industry partners, and will return the favor whenever he calls on me for help. I've since recommended him to several of my colleagues, and a year later, I did visit his property and subsequently recommended it in a SPIN newsletter. All because he was selfless and not pushy in a simple LinkedIn invitation a year prior.

eMail

Email is not going away anytime soon, and although it is not as well received as LinkedIn messages these days, it's still an excellent communication tool if used correctly. Planners typically ignore mass email blasts unless the information is immediately relevant for one of their events. Some may file them away for future use, if they save them at all.

Still, these emails are easy and cheap, so it does not hurt to use blasts occasionally to catch the low-hanging fruit. Just do not overdo it. I get a weekly email blast from a property in another part of the world that I have no intention of booking. A colleague of mine gets a *daily* email from a supplier! This is beyond promotion to the point of annoying their audience. Monthly or semi-monthly is about right, unless there's valuable content beyond your property updates and sales team promotions.

A. Mass eMail Blasts

When you send out mass emails via mail-merge to appear as if you just sent it to each of us personally, we usually can tell, because they are written like a business letter, with no personalization. One way to increase your success rate is to personalize the first sentence (which also can be done via mail merge!).

This simple act does take a little time, but I challenge you to a test: send out 100 emails via regular mail merge with just the greeting line personalized (Dear Bob). Then send the same email to 100 different planners, with the first sentence customized, and compare your results. How should you customize? Take one minute per planner to visit their LinkedIn profile for some common link you can mention. Simple as that.

How to Customize Your eMail Merge

1. Using your existing spreadsheet of contacts, add a column called "Custom."

2. Visit each planner's LinkedIn profile and note something you have in common, or something you found interesting.

First	email	custom
Sara	sara@email.com	we both know Sue Jones.
Shawna	shawna@email.com	we both are originally from Colorado.
Tracey	tracey@email.com	You spoke at WEC last year – great show!

3. Next, create your letter in Word using the step-by-step mail merge wizard (location varies based on your version of Word).

Planner Pet Peeves

4. Insert a greeting field, i.e. Dear [First],

5. Start the letter with: "I was just visiting your LinkedIn profile and noticed that [custom]. The merge will input the custom phrase that you pulled from each planner's unique profile, making them feel like you're writing just to them.

6. Continue your letter casually. "I wanted to let you know that if you need something in Michigan, I'm your guy. Please keep me in mind if I can be a resource, whether you book my property or not."

7. TIP: Choose your subject line carefully! If it's boring, generic or too salesy, you've defeated all that extra work and your email will be perceived as junk. My suggestion: ask a question. "Can We Connect?" or state "Saw Your LinkedIn Profile" in the subject line. Who wouldn't be curious?

"It has to have an interesting subject line to get me to read it," said Linda Hurtley, Meeting Planner, The Linwood Group in Minneapolis. "Maybe tell me what they can do for me."

B. One More eMail Success Tip

I face the same challenges as you. I am tasked every quarter with reaching out to a couple thousand or so of our members to let them know of upcoming member events in their cities. My response rate was low until I changed one simple thing: the subject line. I changed it from a generic subject to a question: "Can You Attend?" My response rate soared to over 80% on average per city, because every planner thought I was reaching out to them personally.

So figure out a way to change your mundane subject line ('XYZ Hotel Announces $10M Renovation!') into a question ('Can I get your opinion on our renovation?'), and you will have a much better chance of breaking through all the clutter and getting your message read.

C. Yet Another eMail Success Tip

Planners love to be asked for advice. Why not ask us for input on the very things you're doing to try to attract planners? Some planners may not have the time or interest to respond, but those with a true interest in your product, services or destination will be honored and many will take the time to respond.

Ask us if the new ad campaign's tag line appeals to planners. Ask us if we could give you input on your new product line, décor, renovations, whatever you have in the hopper. Ask us what trade shows you should invest in next year. Rather than just blast a mass email after the fact, why not involve us along the way? We'll tell you exactly what appeals to us, and we'll feel more involved, which means emotional buy-in.

This is exactly what social media has taught marketing departments in the last few years: your customers want to be part of the process. If you involve us, not only will you get insight into how we think and what we prefer, but voila, you've just created a bunch of budding new relationships in the process.

D. eNewsletters

Are suppliers' electronic newsletters worth the time and effort? That depends entirely on the content. I've learned that case studies get planners' attention. Include a case study showing how one of our fellow planners did something interesting at your property, or how you solved their problem with your service, and we'll take notice.

Section II: Building Relationships

A company out of Minneapolis sends out a quarterly newsletter full of case studies and photos, and I read it from cover-to-cover every time. It is not sent out too frequently, and it contains great solutions that other planners have used in their events, with a soft sell on how the supplier company was involved. Had they instead simply filled their newsletter with articles about how great they are, and how Marcia is now VP of sales, I honestly would not read it.

Another great e-Newsletter that I read regularly is also out of Minnesota. It is full of tips on how planners can take care of their health, manage stress, learn about new tech trends, and also has some fun tips each quarter as well. It talks to us like we are people first and planners second - fantastic and unique!

E. Websites

It may surprise you to hear that many of us do not read your lengthy proposals or marketing materials. When we receive a proposal, we pick out the five or six key items and file the rest away. If you send us a catalog, we file it away, if we save it at all. These days, most planners prefer to go straight to your web site as a form of one-stop shopping, where we

Planner Pet Peeves

hope to find everything we need. It is fantastic when venue web sites have a virtual tour, in addition to the expected floor plans and capacity charts. Most of all, everything needs to be easy to find.

If you're a small supplier and want to stand out, how about a simple YouTube video on your home page with straight talk about how you are different? Nothing elaborate or expensive is needed, just an honest message about how you do business differently and why we should choose you. It humanizes your business and your staff to us.

If you are unsure how your web site stacks up, or if you are ready for a web site redesign, here is an idea for you. Pose the question in a LinkedIn group, asking planners to visit your site and share candid feedback about how to make it better.

Alternately, you could create a small focus group of planners who have done business with you, mixed with those you wish would book with you. It can be in person or via conference call. This is a great excuse to get a group of planners to go to lunch with you! You will get honest advice and build relationships at the same time.

Section II: Building Relationships

Remember, in general, we love to be asked for help and advice, time permitting.

Planner Pet Peeves

CHAPTER 4.

Snail Mail

A few years ago, I would have cautioned you against print mailings due to the stigma against non-"green" promotions. Although that stigma still exists, you can achieve some great results because the volume of mail planners used to receive is now down to a trickle. You'll definitely stand out if you do it right.

Planner Pet Peeves

So how do you do it right?

- Eco-friendly paper and printing are great.

- Hand-written envelopes almost always get read. I know you know this, but it bears repeating since so few do it. It's a time-consuming hassle, but it really does pay off. If you don't have the time, find an intern, trade for services, or hire a retiree.

- If the return address is from a person rather than a company, you have a better chance of getting your mail read.

- Also, I have a theory about 'lumpy mail.' Nobody throws it away. You could include the most mundane sales material, and if you throw in a mint, a pen (or better yet, a branded iPad stylus!), i.e. something 'lumpy,' I believe your chances of getting it opened and read are close to 99.999%.

- Don't use an outdated database! A planner friend of mine receives multiple copies of the same mailings sent to a half-dozen employees who have been off his payroll for years. If you're not using a database that's cleaned at least once a year, especially in this economy rife with turnover, you're doing more harm than good.

- Don't waste your money on printed catalogs of your properties anymore. I bet if you did a small survey of your database, most planners would request that information electronically. Then it is up to you to follow the email tips to make sure it gets read. Why not include some event case studies featuring real planners in your usual annual directory? It will be more appealing and we are more likely to read it and keep it.

Use Snail Mail to Humanize Your Sales Force

Another great way to connect with planners is to send out something unique. One great example comes from a major supplier of an electronic registration system. How do they stand out to me and countless other planners?

They send out an annual holiday cookbook, with each member of their team submitting a

Planner Pet Peeves

recipe and photo of themselves holding their dish. Each employee from the I.T. Department to the C.E.O. participates, and includes a little back-story about the recipe without taking themselves too seriously.

I recall a recipe for something like hot cocoa that included a packet of Swiss Miss and water, from one of their less-culinary team members. Not only does something like this stand out from every other newsletter or holiday greeting we receive, we tell other planners about it. A great idea can translate into a lot of goodwill and viral marketing if it's not the usual thing that we see every day.

Section II: Building Relationships

CHAPTER 5.

Networking

Networking is one of the few things that have not changed much in recent years. There is still the usual mix of trade shows, monthly industry meetings, sales trips, annual awards events, etc. The way we network at these events hasn't changed much. As a result, I don't have a litany of pet peeves to share with you (I heard you sigh with relief). Instead, I will share some tips from planners, and some good networking ideas I've picked up from other suppliers.

Sales Trips

We planners are people-pleasers by nature, as I have mentioned. I was asked by a new acquaintance for help connecting her with my colleagues as she prepared to visit my city during a sales trip. I was happy to help – I emailed a bunch of my colleagues and introduced them to my new supplier friend. I really can't explain why I hopped into action to do this, except that I'm rarely asked by suppliers for help, and she needed help. I think there are a lot of planners like this out there. Sometimes you just have to ask, and share with us that you need some help.

Local Chapter Events

I love to introduce newcomers around at various industry association events. I remember how it felt to be the newcomer, and it can be difficult to network among established cliques.

If you are planning to attend an event where you anticipate knowing nobody, use LinkedIn. See which connections of yours might be willing to make an introduction to one of their colleagues who will be attending. Then ask that person if they wouldn't mind introducing you around. I'd be surprised if they said no.

The Pop-In

Are you guilty of the office pop-in? This is where a supplier shows up without an appointment and hopes to have a few minutes of a planner's time. Do not do this. The planner may come and see you out of obligation, but she will grumble all the way back to her desk, even if you brought cookies. When planners are hard at work and 'in the zone' on a project or two, having an unplanned appointment can throw us off. If you feel like you must do the office pop-in anyway, try calling ahead and saying, "Hey, I'm in the neighborhood, can I drop off our new brochure and some coffee or a snack in a few minutes?"

Coffee Talk

I know it's harder these days for suppliers to get planners out of the office for lunch, or even coffee. Planners have told me that an appointment that kills two birds with one stone is more attractive.

Planner Pet Peeves

You can make your coffee appointment more attractive if you combine it with the opportunity for us to network with colleagues. That means arranging a small group coffee and inviting a handful of us. As I suggested previously, if you tell one of us what you're planning and ask us for help identifying others to invite, we're likely to help, if we have the time. Don't feel awkward telling us exactly the type of planners you're looking to meet: corporate, independent, government, international, etc.

This means that for the price of a few coffees, you'll have some decently pre-qualified leads who will come to have coffee, meet you, and catch up with colleagues. The gathering will take on a more social feel, and you'll build better relationships and goodwill compared to a typical sales appointment.

The Dog Park

If budgets are tight and you want to do something unique and fun, here's a great idea I heard from a supplier. She invites planners for a doggy play date at the local dog park! What a fantastic idea. It's something you can do in the evening or on a weekend. It immediately humanizes you and lowers our defenses, and we all get to hang out and meet each other's dogs. She invites several planners to do this each time, so again they have the added attraction to come and network with colleagues as well. You could post an invitation for a Doggy Mixer in one or two local LinkedIn discussion groups, and see who shows up. Don't have a dog? Borrow one!

The Client Event

If your company hosts an annual event for current and prospective clients, here are some ideas from your target audience. Busy planners have told me that they prefer to visit multiple companies in one trip, so if you can combine your event to feature a few non-competing companies, planners will find it more attractive to attend. It is a more efficient use of their time if they can see multiple vendors rather than just one.

If you're a production company, you could join forces with a décor company, an entertainment company, and maybe a speaker's bureau. The other good news, besides boosting your attendance, is you can share the costs among several companies rather than just footing the bill by yourself.

If you can offer some sort of education at your event, all the better. Planners really need to justify attending your event, especially if it is held during work hours, and an educational component helps us do that for our bosses, and ourselves. It doesn't have to cost a lot. Bring in a local chef, a behind-the-scenes production specialist, an attorney, or a hotel RevPar manager – all of whom would probably speak for free. Make sure their information isn't a sales pitch, but rather something of value. Attendees will be more likely to tell other planners about it afterward, and they'll be sure to make time for it the next time around as well.

The In-Transition Support Group

There always are planners out there who are in-transition, especially during the latest recession. Many have told me how the phone simply stops ringing, and the invitations quit coming. It is really unfortunate and a bit short-sighted, especially with senior-level planners. You know they are going to land on their feet, and their next position will probably have as much buying power as their previous one. Who do you think they will stay loyal to? The suppliers who dropped them like a hot potato, or the one who says, "Hey, I'm having a little meet-up for a group of colleagues who are in-transition, and I'd love to have you join us. I'll buy the coffee, you just come for the camaraderie." Wow – you've just won huge points with that whole group, again for the price of a few beverages. You can bet they will be forever grateful, and hold you in high regard as someone who offered support during a challenging time.

Planner Pet Peeves

Section II: Building Relationships

CHAPTER 6.

Trade Shows & Hosted Buyer Events

I was recently asked by a supplier, "How do we get planners to stop by our booth, and how do we get them to like us right away?"

That's the million-dollar question that every exhibitor asks themselves. You're making a huge investment of money and time, and it needs to bring you the proper return on investment, otherwise why bother?

My answer to her was to offer chocolate or charity. We'll definitely stop to chat if doing so will help a charity, or get us some chocolate. Otherwise, as you know, we tend to try not to make eye contact.

Are Trade Shows on the Way Out?

"It seems like with every trade show I go to, the value seems to be less and less," said Daphne Meyers, CMM, Events Marketing Specialist with AE2S in North Dakota. "I think there needs to be a revamp, as many exhibitors feel they have to be there, but attendees aren't really interested in doing business that way."

Trade shows have definitely lost some popularity, as both suppliers and planners are starting to favor hosted buyer events where they are paired for one-on-one appointments over the course of the event.

Still, I believe there is a good case for trade shows. I know many of us like to walk a trade show floor to get ideas. The problem is that exhibitor traffic is getting lighter and lighter, whether that is due to the economy, or the format. The result is that many planners have said they feel like a piece of meat. Many turn their badges around so their 'planner' ribbon doesn't show, so they can walk around in peace. I know that's terrible, but it's the truth.

I have experienced both extremes. Usually, I attend shows as a planner and get lots of attention from suppliers as I stroll the aisles of a trade show. In 2011, I walked the first AIBTM show in Baltimore with a media badge (I was writing about the new show for the SPIN newsletter). Nobody...and I mean *nobody*... initiated a conversation with me as I walked down the aisles for an entire day, unless it was someone I already knew. I loved it because I could really cover the entire huge show floor and take in all the different destinations without constant interruption. That sounds harsh – I know exhibitors have a tough job to get our attention, but I don't want to waste your time or mine if I know a destination just isn't going to work.

Hosted Buyer Events

Have you noticed the large increase in hosted buyer events lately? They're a fairly new concept so there's some novelty that's attractive to both planners and suppliers. They're also increasing in number because they work. Planners who are short on time can get

Planner Pet Peeves

in, meet exactly the suppliers they want to meet, and get out. Suppliers like them because every appointment is an interested lead that justifies the supplier's investment in the event.

I have to warn you though, that the number of shows is approaching critical mass, and at some point the novelty will wear off with planners. That means that not every event will be able to attract the right number or mix of planners to justify your participation going forward. We may already be at that point.

Also, many of these appointment-only events tend to be held in alluring destinations like Florida, which is hard for planners to justify sometimes to the boss. Even with all our expenses paid, sometimes it's also hard to justify unless the show offers an educational component.

Hosted buyer events will lose some popularity as the glut of events outpaces the interest of planner participants. Nevertheless, the ones with a strong following will survive and thrive. Just choose wisely – ask some of your planner friends what they think, or post in a LinkedIn discussion board and ask our opinion about this event or that. Remember, we love that.

Hybrid Events

I really like the two new hybrid shows that came to North America in 2011: AIBTM and IMEX. Each offers a combination trade show and hosted buyer event, which is the best of both worlds. I know these shows are extremely expensive for suppliers without deep pockets, so I really hope they get the ROI they need to continue participating.

Both shows have paired up with strong education partners: AIBTM with PCMA, and IMEX with MPI. There's no discounting the value of these educational programs to draw planners to attend.

Planner Pet Peeves

Section II: Building Relationships

CHAPTER 7.

Advertising

I have some friends who work at the industry magazines, and they will not like what I'm about to share. Traditional print advertising is gasping its last breath. This is no surprise to those friends of mine – they already know it. SPIN surveyed our planner members a year ago to ask them about their current magazine reading habits. The most popular response is that the magazines pile up until the planners have a chance to read them on airplanes. That means two things: 1) planners still find the content of those magazines worth saving and

Planner Pet Peeves

hauling on a trip, and 2) they will only read magazines these days if they cannot get online.

The smart publications have been looking into alternative ways to reach planners and serve their advertisers. Most industry magazines these days have an electronic version, which is fantastic. I open them and leave them open in my browser to peruse when I get a break in the action here and there.

What's the point? Print advertisers need to start considering the fact that circulation numbers are not what they seem these days. I have a dozen magazines each month that I never get to, plus extra copies for former employees that still keep coming years later. So that circulation promise of 10,000 readers really isn't accurate.

I know your marketing dollars are precious, so just be aware of what planners are really doing and how much ROI you're really getting with print advertising, and consider a shift to digital advertising with those same magazines.

Social Media

Social media has been in the limelight now for a few years as the new 'it' medium for companies to reach customers. It works with varying degrees of success, depending on the strategy used by the company. To reach potential SPIN members, I rely strictly on LinkedIn as my social medium of choice, because my demographic doesn't hang out on Facebook or Twitter. Many large corporations don't even allow their employees to access certain social sites at work. It's therefore important to target your social media on sites where your potential customers actually spend time.

It's also important to use social media the way your customers use it. Those who use Facebook, LinkedIn and Twitter to blast out sales messages have missed the point. Social media is about making real connections, having conversations, and about empowering your audience to be your brand ambassadors.

There's a statistic I like to share in my webinars: nearly 80% of consumers trust businesses less than just one year ago. They trust their peers for honest feedback on your company – they don't trust what you have to say about your company anymore. It isn't about talking *at* your customers anymore; it's about talking *with* them, or enabling them to talk with each other about you.

The whole key to social media is to create raving fans and provide a forum for them to connect with each other to discuss you. If you don't know how to do social media properly, hire someone who does, because it's not going away. Facebook and Twitter will be replaced someday by whatever is the next big thing, but the empowerment of customers is here to stay.

Web Site Advertising

In my opinion, web site advertising is challenging. In today's media-glutted world, consumers have almost been trained to overlook the ads, precisely because they are everywhere. We tune them out. I didn't even know Facebook had advertising until a couple years ago when someone had to point it out to me. Still, not all web site advertising is bad. If the page isn't too cluttered with competing images, and your ad is creative, your investment is probably worth it. Again, here's where a planner focus group would really pay off, and many planners will gladly help you out over coffee or lunch – it doesn't have to be formal or structured.

Section II: Building Relationships

CHAPTER 8.

Sponsorships – Do They Matter?

Suppliers invest a lot of money on sponsorships of countless industry events: golf tournaments, chapter education days, annual association conferences, and many, many more. Does it make a difference? Does it have the anticipated effect with planners? The senior-level planners had some great feedback on this topic.

Most senior-level planners have served on a committee for an industry association at some point in their career. They know what it takes

Planner Pet Peeves

to produce a chapter event or fund raiser, and they understand how vital sponsors are. For anybody who has been on the committee side of an industry event, the appreciation for what sponsors provide is evident and appreciated.

Many planners are tasked with generating sponsorships for their clients' or companies' events as well. They 'get it,' and know the value.

Does that mean that because your logo appears on a sign at a chapter event, you will get our business? Of course not, but it does build goodwill. If you invest in strategic sponsorships that drive more value to your company besides logo exposure, then the impact is much greater.

If you're not seeing the value you need for a particular sponsorship investment, negotiate. It's a sponsorship buyer's market and committees usually are flexible enough to craft a custom package with the components that make sense for your marketing strategy. Of course, it's much easier to negotiate if you're buying more than just the lowest-level sponsorship package.

SECTION III.

Hotels

"The definition of insanity is doing the same thing over and over again and expecting different results."
– Albert Einstein

Planner Pet Peeves

CHAPTER 9.

Apparently I Struck a Nerve...

Recently, I posed a question on the private SPIN member discussion board: 'What is your biggest pet peeve about hotels these days?' Apparently I struck a nerve, because no topic ever has received so many posts in SPIN history. Why?

Well, here's a theory. Regardless of the type of planner (association, corporate, incentive, independent, etc.), we all spend a large amount of time working with—and in—hotels.

Planner Pet Peeves

Within SPIN, the planners average around 20 years in the industry.

Conservatively speaking, if they each plan an average of 15 meetings or events per year, at an average of three nights each, that's nine hundred hotel nights over 20 years. Add to that the nights they spend in hotels for site inspections, familiarization trips, industry conferences and personal vacations, and the average senior-level planner has spent around two thousand nights in hotels over a 20-year career. That works out to about FIVE AND A HALF YEARS they've lived in hotels (2000 nights divided by 365 days per year)! Is it any wonder we've developed a few preferences and opinions along the way?

In the following chapters I will share the most commonly voiced hotel pet peeves.

Section III: Hotels

CHAPTER 10.

The Dreaded RFP Process

Both suppliers and planners have a lot of gripes about the whole RFP process. The biggest complaint voiced over and over from planners is that they do not feel their RFPs are being fully read. They pack a lot of detail into the document and send it off (usually with some ridiculous deadline, granted). Then the calls and emails start coming in, asking them for more information that many say is already inside the RFP they spent so much time crafting. Then once they receive the proposals, many suppliers have not addressed all the needs outlined in the RFP by the planner. Clearly there's a disconnect, and I think I have some answers. But first, read some of the feedback below.

"Hotel sales should pay closer attention to specs on an RFP. If I indicate deluxe king guest rooms, don't give me a rate for standard rooms (specify room types and rates)," said Judy Anderson, CMP from The Nielsen Company in Chicago. "If I request 10-12 feet max meeting room ceiling height, don't propose a section of a ballroom. If I request a U-shape setup, don't put me in a room too narrow."

Now, before you go slamming the book closed and cursing me under your breath, let me say that we planners are guilty. We're guilty of sending you RFPs and imposing overly-demanding deadlines. We're guilty of collecting your proposals and then going 'radio dark' on you for weeks, or even months. Suppliers can't possibly dedicate the time to thoroughly read and thoughtfully respond to every RFP when deadlines aren't reasonable in the first place. I get it. I've also heard *your* complaints from all across North America, every time I bring up the RFP subject.

This situation isn't getting better, it's getting worse. Over the past few years, planners have proven that they can produce meetings in ridiculous time frames, which has caused our bosses and clients to believe that we always should work this quickly. That means they now demand and expect miracles from us on a regular basis. We pass those demands and expectations on to you, and when you come through for us, we then expect you to perform that same miracle on every RFP. The industry is getting more demanding, not less demanding, which means the days of reasonable deadlines are gone forever.

To further complicate this whole process, when planners go through CVBs, the CVB sometimes doesn't attach our original RFP, and you receive only the basic information needed to do a space & rate search. Demand the original, full RFP from your Bureau so you have all the information, because you're the one getting blamed when it's incomplete!

When you receive an RFP, ask us if the deadline is firm or if there is a day or two of wiggle room. More than likely there is – just like everyone else, we often pad our deadlines in case we have latecomers or complications. If you share with us a little about your crazy schedule and why an extra day or two would be tremendously helpful, it does two things: 1) it humanizes you where before you may have just been another supplier on our list, and 2) it reminds us that you're running from pillar to post just like we are.

> ### Some Insight into the RFP Waiting Game
>
> We scurry around to get information in a hurry to our clients or bosses, expecting—and promised—a quick decision. Then they wait, and wait, and stall, and postpone, and stall some more, until we're about to pull our hair out. Meanwhile, you call us and email us for an update, and so does every competitor who received our RFP.
>
> The sheer volume of these 'check-in' calls is staggering considering we're probably working a dozen meetings at once, times five or ten suppliers, meaning at any given time, we're dealing with 60-120 different suppliers. Coupled with the fact that we're not getting answers from our higher-ups, we're frustrated, embarrassed, and time-strapped to reply to the growing number of frustrated suppliers – especially those who ping us more than once or twice for an answer.

Section III: Hotels

If we insist that the deadline is firm, you can always send us a short-form proposal answering our specific requests, and let us know that complete information beyond our wildest dreams can be provided if requested.

As a planner for 20 years, I can tell you that I create a spreadsheet for all the proposals for a given meeting or event, and consolidate all supplier submissions into just five or six columns of key information. If I need further information about your lovely property, I don't comb through your proposal, I go to your website because it's far easier to find what I need quickly. So don't waste your time on quantity of information, focus on quality. Sift through our RFP and make sure our key issues are addressed. We know you use a template to save time, but really, 2-3 pages will suffice. There's no gold star for the supplier who submits the thickest proposal.

Another planner pet peeve is when they receive calls or emails from suppliers who have questions that are clearly answered within the RFP. We know that these suppliers are often just trying to make a human connection to establish rapport, and asking questions usually is a good method to show your interest. Make sure, however, that the questions haven't already been answered or your call will have

Planner Pet Peeves

the opposite effect. Remember, as planners, we're typically very detail-oriented. If you show us right off the bat that you aren't, we will distrust you as a true partner, and this translates into fears that our needs won't be met during critical meeting stages.

> **Proposal Quick Tip**
>
> There are three key questions a supplier can ask that immediately set you apart from the competition and make you stand out to planners—especially senior-level planners.
>
> 1) Ask us if we wouldn't mind sharing the *goals and objectives* of the event. Anyone who's gone through the process to obtain their CMP designation has had this ingrained into their brain for all eternity. Goals and objectives – it's the first thing we address when planning anything. In all my years of planning, I've been asked this only <u>one time</u>, and that was by a supplier who used to be a planner! Wow, was I impressed. If you ask us for this information, it tells us you are of CMP caliber (even if you don't have the designation). It also shows that you care about providing us with relevant information, and positions you as a collaborator in the success of our meeting. Be sure to repeat our goals and objectives back

Section III: Hotels

> to us in the first paragraph of your proposal, to reinforce that you understand us and our meetings.
>
> 2) Ask us about the *demographics* of our group. This will help you understand our hot buttons and give you insight into how to sell your property to us.
>
> 3) Ask us what our *top three priorities* are: rate, space, attrition flexibility, etc. We're telling you exactly how to sell to us! You'll be surprised how candid we will be, and again you project yourself as a meeting partner, not just someone in this for a quick sale.

The final pet peeve I'll share here is about centralized sales offices. When we send an RFP to a particular property in Florida, for example, we don't want to speak to a sales representative in Chicago who never has set foot on the property. This is about relationships, and the concept of centralized sales forces really annoys us.

When a major hotel chain let a number of seasoned salespeople go, in favor of centralized sales, our SPIN private discussion

Planner Pet Peeves

board lit up with angry planners. That was a terrible move – the chain commoditized its own product! It removed the human relationships that ultimately win us over in the end, and keep us coming back.

"That tells me that [unnamed hotel chain] looks at their entire brand as a product, and not a service," said Tracey B. Smith, CMP, CMM, VP of Programming with SPIN in Minnesota. "It's really unfortunate that they are so short-sighted that they see only the bottom line."

Guess who we're loyal to: the salesperson or the property? Over and over again, the planners of SPIN say that if they have a strong relationship with a salesperson, they will follow that salesperson to a different property. If the new property meets our needs, the long-standing relationship with the salesperson means they will get the business, not the former property. Way to go, unnamed hotel chain!

Planners understand that hotels are in the business to make a profit. When one major chain offers us great relationships and another one takes those away and gives us a faceless phone contact, which chain do you think we prefer?

CHAPTER 11.

Site Inspections

I've heard all sorts of interesting site inspection pet peeves from SPIN planners. Some are simply inexcusable, like the property not being aware of your appointment, or a salesperson being completely unprepared. Fortunately, this doesn't happen very often. Other pet peeves run the gamut. I've chosen the most common to share with you.

A. Delegating the Tour

Don't send another sales person to conduct your tour because you're busy. Remember how important relationships are to us, especially planners of a senior-level. If the person showing us around has never spoken with us and flips through a file to learn about our needs while conducting the tour, that's a horrible first impression. You've delegated us to someone else, and that's how we perceive the entire hotel will treat our meeting: as second rate. This is excusable only if you are a) in labor, b) busy preparing an elaborate spa visit for the planner after the tour, c) truly unable to be there and have told us <u>prior</u> to our arrival, or d) sincerely not interested in the business and deliberately want us to go elsewhere.

B. Conducting an Endless Tour

Time is shorter these days for everything, including site inspections. We usually will tell you our time frame for a tour, and if we haven't, please ask. Then I highly suggest you ask us what we want to see, not just take us along on auto-pilot, giving us the same tour you give everyone else. We want to know that our meeting is special, and that you hear us.

I can't tell you how many times I've been on site inspections and the salesperson did not respect my wish list. I'm a strange bird: if I'm on a tight schedule, I always tell the salesperson I don't want to see the spa or any suites, because it's a proven fact that only .0001 percent of spas and suites are undesirable (If it's an incentive program, of course I need to see those things, but otherwise, it's not as important).

I know they're your showpieces, but I'm there to get down to business and see what is truly going to differentiate you from the competition for a particular meeting. About eighty percent of the time, I am dragged to the spa "just for a peek" and "just one suite" anyway, cutting short my time to really see what I came for, which could be your outdoor event space, your breakout sessions, the chef, and what-not.

C. Not Respecting Our Time

If we say we only have an hour for your tour, we mean it. Then it's even more critical to prioritize exactly what we want to see, and what we don't. If we're only there for a board meeting, don't show us the ballroom, and vice-versa. Like dating, we usually know if it's a good match in the first ten minutes anyway (tough crowd, I know)!

> **Quick Tip**
>
> Ask us if we want to see the same room category configured as a king and then see it as a double-double. If you have several different room categories, this is even more important. Most of us will say not to waste your time (we really mean our time), because we can envision the exact same room with different beds in it. Really.

I recently went on a whirlwind tour of hotels in a major city. Time was limited, and we literally had no more than an hour to spend at each hotel. Of the six properties we toured that day, five of them did not respect this time limit. 'Just one more room,' or 'you really have to see the view from the Presidential Suite,' again and again. We never want to be rude, but in some cases we had to be extremely direct with the salesperson just get out the door. The one property that won my respect was the one where the salesperson said, "I know we have just an hour, so tell me what you want to see the most, in order of priority, and I'll do my best." She kept glancing at her watch during the tour and giving us updates: "We still have 15 minutes left, we're doing great!" Which salesperson do you think I want to work with the most?

D. How a Thoughtful Room Amenity Can Backfire

Tracy Stuckrath, CSEP, CMM, CHC, is President of *Thrive! Meetings and Events* out of Atlanta. In my opinion, she's the foremost planner expert on food and beverage issues in our industry. "Know your planners' likes and dislikes and any food allergies," Stuckrath advises. "When a welcome gift arrives to our room and the planner can't eat it because of a dietary need or a dislike, you've wasted money, time and food and made your gift not so welcoming. Offering them something you know they will enjoy goes a lot further and adds that special touch."

E. Site Inspections Done Right

Here are some tips for you that I've picked up from other planners over the years:

- One planner spoke of her love for her dogs, and when she checked into her room, the salesperson had arranged a gift basket *for her dogs*. It contained all sorts of goodies for her to bring home for her beloved pets. It blew her away and she has since shared the story with countless colleagues about the experience. We always appreciate the thought when you deliver a welcome gift to our room. If you go a step further and figure out what we're passionate about, it really shows that you will go the extra mile, and is the beginning (or continuation) of a great relationship.

- Room gifts don't have to be elaborate or expensive (and if they are, it makes many of us uncomfortable). I've brought a number of groups over the years to The Lodge at Torrey Pines. They have little bowls of kumquats in the guest rooms during kumquat season. I had never tried one before, but during one stay, I sampled one. I commented about how hard it was to peel the little bugger (turns out you eat them whole). Now whenever I stay there, or when their sales team comes to Minnesota, there's always a special delivery of kumquats just for me. It's an inside joke that always reminds me how great their team is and that I'm not just a number to them.

- Another planner told of a tour she took of a Phoenix resort property with her client. At several points along the tour, random hotel staff (bellman, maid, etc.) greeted the planner and her client <u>by name</u> and welcomed them to the resort. The tour ended out at the poolside bar, where the bartender had perfectly timed it to deliver beverages and thank them by name for visiting. Very impressive!

- The chef plays an important role in setting your property apart. Ask the planner if meeting the chef is important. On a site visit to Los Cabos, the chef at one of the resorts brought my client and me to his office and poured us some high-end tequila and gave us a lesson in assessing different types. Granted, it was ten o'clock in the morning, but the special treatment left an impression with my client.

- I'll let you in on a little secret: planners love to feel like they're getting special

VIP access to places that are normally off-limits to us. If you take us on a back-of-house tour or through the kitchen (provided those areas are up-to-par), we feel special. If you're doing renovations or building a new property, offer us a hard-hat tour! You may not want to show the property until it's completely finished, but we really feel like we're experiencing something before everyone else, which we love. We'll talk it up to our colleagues, guaranteed. I still fondly remember a hard-hat tour of The Bellagio in Las Vegas before it opened.

- The more senior-level the planner, the less we want to hear your property's features and benefits. We want to hear strategic solutions to serve our clients and make us look like rock stars in the process. That's the key to the kingdom.

- Lastly, you'll win big points if you help us envision what other planners have done with your property. Especially for senior-level planners, we get burned out sometimes and it's hard to constantly churn out creative ideas. We love to hear what others have done that were especially creative or impressive. You know your property best, so help us to see possibilities from basic to outlandish (depending on the group demographics, of course).

Planner Pet Peeves

CHAPTER 12.

Contracts

Most of our pet peeves about contracts have to do with all the nickel-and-dime fees that hotels try to put into them, but more on that later. First, there are a couple issues that aren't fee-related.

A. Does Anyone Out There Actually Read Them?

According to the majority of planners I've surveyed, there's a big disconnect between the sales department and the billing department. Planners tell me that a perfectly accurate bill is like the legendary Chupacabra or the Loch Ness Monster: we might believe they exist, but most of us have never seen one.

Most of us prefer a daily billing review during a multi-day event to minimize inaccuracies. This normally applies just to the accumulating charges like F&B and A/V. It's the things we don't approve on a daily basis that get muddled along the way. The inaccuracies usually come from room block credits, negotiated concessions and other items that are outside the norm or specific only to our group. If your company or property has done a stellar job and really impressed us, please don't ruin that last impression by making us sift through a lengthy final bill full of errors.

B. The IATA Debacle

A few years back, an unnamed large hotel chain decided it would be a brilliant Idea to require planners to obtain an IATA (International Air Transport Association) accreditation in order to collect commissions. Last time I checked, I was a meeting planner, not a travel agent. Most of us never book air, so why should we be accredited by IATA to

Section III: Hotels

prove we are planners? The process is time-consuming and not cheap. This created a *huge* firestorm on our SPIN discussion board, and planners continue to gripe about it to this day.

For any other hotel chains considering following suit, read on. The following quotes are recent selections from SPIN's member discussion board – clearly we're still angry about this, and it's not going away.

"I understand that [Hotel Company] needs to have a way to "flush out" the professionals from the posers --- but I do not understand why they feel the need discount our entire profession! Event managers are not travel agents; we have our OWN trade associations. Why couldn't they have come up with a qualification system to validate us and our profession?" asks Loretta Lowe, CMP, an independent senior-level planner from San Francisco. "I do not work on commission; but I stand behind those event and meeting professionals who do. I feel very strongly that [Hotel Company] did us an injustice. Unfortunately, it seems like our profession is always having to defend our existence."

She's not alone - here's another one:

Planner Pet Peeves

"Requiring IATA numbers as a tool to pay third-party meeting planners their commission: The International Air Transport Association (IATA) is its global trade organization," said Jane Kooiman, Director of Meeting Services for Equinox Creative in Minnesota. "It has nothing to do with booking hotel rooms and should have nothing to do with [nameless hotel chain]'s ability to pay planners the commission for sourcing space. I hope that [unnamed hotel chain] revisits this procedure very soon!"

If there's any doubt left in your mind about whether requiring IATA numbers is a good idea for your hotel chain, here's one last thought for you:

"I got an IATA number, but I resent having to," said Bonni Scepkowski, President and CEO, Stellar Meetings and Events out of New Jersey. "[Unnamed hotel chain] should make arrangements through MPI or another meeting organization. We're not interchangeable with travel agencies. I don't like having to pay to belong to an organization that I don't need (not to mention the small fact that they sell our email/phone and fax numbers. I'm inundated with faxes from travel consolidators/etc. Very annoying). What am I paying for? I don't get the benefits that travel agents get (discounted airfare, etc.). I'm literally paying to get paid."

Section III: Hotels

Another great move, [unnamed hotel chain]. Next time you make a sweeping move like this, let's pose the question to our SPIN members. You'll have unabashed feedback and won't risk alienating an entire segment of the industry.

Planner Pet Peeves

CHAPTER 13.

Fees, Fees, Ridiculous Fees

If the last decade was about relationships, I believe the next decade in our industry is about relationships + transparency. Nobody likes to feel like they've been duped, and that's how planners feel when we uncover hidden costs after we've gone to contract. A week before the event (or worse yet, on site at the event), we learn that there's a fee to turn on the air conditioning, or to breathe air in the outdoor venue space, or some other ridiculous charge dreamed up by a Revenue Manager.

Planner Pet Peeves

While those examples obviously are exaggerations, I'm constantly amazed at new charges that pop up, and there's no way the planner could possibly anticipate such preposterous things during the contract phase. The result? We feel 'had,' and we now have to face our boss or client and explain the budget overage. The hotel has made a buck, but at what expense? Planners *hate* surprise charges and *loathe* being made to look foolish in front of our higher-ups. As a result, we tell many, many colleagues about the negative experience.

What fees generate the most complaints from my planner colleagues?

- **Internet access** has got to be number one these days. Many properties have compromised and now offer free Wi-Fi in the lobby, but not in the meeting space or the guest rooms. Many of us wonder why we pay $12 to connect our laptop in our guest room, but the same laptop connection costs $750 in the ballroom.

    Some properties charge a per-device fee rather than a per-room fee, meaning if someone has an iPad, a

Section III: Hotels

laptop and a Kindle, I have to justify to him why he has to pay three access charges per day. SPIN member Rosie Ledesma-Bernaducci, CMP of McVeigh Associates out of New Jersey adds: "Charging per Internet device...ya kidding?! Why does a huge hotel chain charge but then the Comfort Inns don't? I don't get that!?" I hear this *all the time* from colleagues.

- Service charges have gotten out of control, with some properties charging 28% and little or none of that ever makes it into the pockets of the hard-working servers. We have to give gratuities on top of that 28% to reward those people ourselves. Believe me, this is a huge point of contention with planners right now, and we see it as a matter of corporate greed and properties not taking care of their own employees. If employees actually received the entire service fee, as we believe they should, this would be far more palatable for us (although 28% is ridiculous under any circumstances). "One thing that just happened to me...it really irritated me that I didn't catch it in the contract. I had a hotel charge me a service charge *on meeting room rental*. It really burned me. It's just not right," said Linda Hurtley, Meeting Planner at The Linwood Group in Minneapolis.

- **Resort fees.** "Ridiculous surcharges for a paper I don't care about, coffee I don't drink and a health club I don't have time to use," says Kathy Felber, co-owner of Equinox Creative out of Minnesota.

    Carroll Reuben, CMP, CMM of Meeting Excellence out of L.A., adds: "Let's face it, hotels are simply following the example of the airlines; they charge separately for anything and everything. Internet connections, parking - next they'll be charging us for the use of the coffee pot in the room." Note to Revenue Managers: ignore that last part, it was NOT a suggestion!

- **A/V surcharges** when we don't use the in-house A/V company. "I'm now seeing 22% surcharges on all outside A/V brought into the hotel," said Mark Lorimer, CMP, Owner, Eventive Group in Southern California. Believe me,

> many of us would love the convenience of using the on-site company, but we can't justify paying double or triple what an outside vendor charges—especially with today's extreme budget scrutiny and slashing. If their pricing were more competitive to begin with, they'd get more volume!

This anonymous planner sums it all up perfectly:

"We understand that hotels have to make money...they are a for-profit business. I think what many of us are peeved about is that we are trying to create meeting budgets that are realistic. We just need to know up front (without having to be Sherlock Holmes) what we are going to be charged so that we can do that."

Planner Pet Peeves

CHAPTER 14.

Convention Service Managers

Let me say first and foremost that most CSMs work their tails off and do everything within their power to make our meetings and events a success. I believe it's by far the most challenging job in our industry. The good ones are the first ones there in the morning and the last to leave at the end of the day. They work nights and weekends, and when we get to go home and recover from our exhaustion, they go to work the next day juggling several new meetings.

| Planner Pet Peeves |

We know that like everyone else in our industry, CSMs are doing more with less. Juggling more meetings, more planners, more demands. I've got nothing but respect for those in this role. The following pet peeves are geared more toward those who supervise and schedule CSMs.

- Most of my colleagues prefer to deal with CSMs of a similar experience level. If a senior-level planner is working with a junior-level CSM, the planner sometimes feels like she is in a training or mentoring role. During a meeting we need 100% of our focus to be on our own duties. In contrast, a junior-level planner placed with a senior-level CSM probably would feel intimidated. Whenever possible, it would be great to create pairings based on experience level.

- CSMs are our lifeline, our single point of contact at a meeting. If they are scheduled to go on vacation, or have to miss any part of our event, this is extremely aggravating. We know they are entitled to vacation days, but please don't do this in the middle of our events. Don't pass the baton to another CSM unless our assigned CSM is 1) deathly ill, 2) bleeding from the head, or 3) imprisoned. As my sweet, soft-spoken grandmother once surprisingly said to me, "Don't change horses in the middle of the stream – you'll always get screwed."

Planner Pet Peeves

CHAPTER 15.

Hotel Food & Beverage

There are some wonderfully progressive chefs in our industry: those who really embrace the 'locavore' movement to buy as many locally grown items as possible; those who have adapted their purchasing to include more organic items; and those who have made great strides toward healthier menus to serve the growing population with dietary restrictions.

There also are some challenging chefs who are less than happy to work within your budget or get a little creative to match your theme, and that's unfortunate.

Beyond Chicken and Green Beans

We know the catering department is a profitable one for hotels. We understand that they need to provide options that appeal to the masses and have high profitability. Perhaps there's a lack of variety and healthier options because planners aren't willing to pay more for them. Perhaps the burden falls more on planners to demand more than stuffed chicken breast with green beans. I'm not sure which needs to come first: the chicken (no pun intended) or the egg, but a lot of planners would love to see more variety. I hope that planners would be willing to pay more for gluten-free, organic or locavore meals because of the understandably higher costs of the ingredients. Perhaps one of the hotel chains out there will have a focus group about this very subject to foster change.

Dietary Needs at the Forefront

Tracy Stuckrath, CSEP, CMM, CHC, is President of *Thrive! Meetings and Events* out of Atlanta. In my opinion, she's the foremost planner expert on food and beverage issues in our industry. She recently shared an interesting statistic: approximately 50% of attendees these days have dietary needs.

Dietary issues are not to be taken lightly anymore.

"In 2008, the Americans with Disabilities Act was amended," explains Stuckrath. "The immune system and digestive tract were added to the disabilities list to make it clearer what is covered under the ADA as far as food allergies and dietary needs. In the past, eating wasn't specifically called out on that. If somebody has a food allergy or a medical condition that requires them to eat a certain way to survive, they are now covered under the ADA.

"It's not just about the attendee in the wheelchair that needs to have access, it's about the attendee with Celiac Disease, Cancer, Diabetes, Diverticulitis who now has to be treated specially as well," she explained.

I don't believe most planners know this. We usually ask during registration for attendees to identify dietary restrictions, but up until now, I believe it's been primarily for liability reasons, empathy because we have had personal experience with such restrictions, or simply out of kindness. Now it's outlined in the ADA. If attendees disclose that they have certain dietary needs, we as planners and the hotels and caterers we work with need to address those by law.

"Coordinate with your planner how you are going to identify those with the specific dietary needs in a discreet yet effective way," suggests Stuckrath.

She offers this tip to hotel kitchens: "Chefs not only need to prepare the meals, they need to put attendee names on them. This prevents those meals from mistakenly getting into the wrong hands, or going to a late registrant who notifies the planner on-site that they have a dietary need, and my meal goes to them instead, when I pre-requested that meal."

Meeting Breaks

Don't even get me started on break foods. I hope I never see another leaden-brick 'granola bar' (you know the ones with the green wrappers that a table saw has challenges getting through). Sadly, I suspect I will see them until the day I die (probably from one falling on my head).

Section III: Hotels

Here's another opportunity to really showcase organic, gluten-free and locally-produced items. The Lodge at Torrey Pines produces wonderful homemade granola. It's a staple at any event I have there, and I love it so much, I bring a jar home with me. I suspect many of their guests do the same, and it's not cheap. It's become one of the Lodge's signature items. It would be great if every hotel chef had the opportunity to do something like this.

"I had a hotel tell me recently that they need my food order two weeks in advance because they had to order the food. Really?" questioned Sharon L. Schenk, CMP, founder of Your Meeting Professional in Connecticut. "This is a 1,000-room hotel with 80,000 square feet of meeting space. I was also told I couldn't order granola bars on consumption, because they had to be ordered in advance. It's them coming up with new rules that I haven't heard in 18 years that bothers me."

If you're a hotel with a progressive chef who's doing something unique, I encourage you to include a meeting with the chef in your site visits. Even if we're not big foodies ourselves, it's always impressive to learn when a chef grows his own herbs, visits local farmers' markets to buy produce in season, or loves to work with special menus.

Planner Pet Peeves

Also, if we've booked an event with your property, it's always great to be able to speak with the chef directly, rather than having everything interpreted by the CSM and relayed to the chef.

SECTION IV:

Non-Hotel Suppliers

"Even those who fancy themselves the most progressive will fight against other kinds of progress, for each of us is convinced that our way is the best way."
— Louis L'Amour, *The Lonely Men*

Planner Pet Peeves

Section IV: Non-Hotel Suppliers

CHAPTER 16.

It's the Little Things...

There are so many categories of non-hotel suppliers, many of which I chose not to include. Suppliers like décor companies, production houses, florists and the like do not have major pet peeves associated with the entire vendor type – usually it's just a one-off problem that a planner has with late delivery or poor service that applies only to a particular vendor.

The pet peeves for those categories are very general:

Planner Pet Peeves

"I think overall my pet peeves with [certain] vendors are: lack of response once they have the business; when they don't pay attention to details they are sent; and when they're not available during the event when you need them," said Daphne Meyers, CMM, Events Marketing Specialist with AE2S out of North Dakota.

Read on for some feedback from planners on categories where they do have an occasional (or frequent) challenge.

CHAPTER 17.

Convention & Visitors Bureaus

I'm a little biased about working with CVBs, because I've never had a bad experience in 20 years of planning. I am surprised when I meet planners who either have never used a Convention & Visitors Bureau, or got burnt once and believe all CVBs are bad. There are, unfortunately, a handful of CVBs out there who still do things that give a bad rep to the rest of the wonderful ones out there. Here are some of the pet peeves I've heard from my colleagues:

Planner Pet Peeves

- If you read the RFP section earlier in this book, you know that we hate incomplete proposals from hotels. We blame the hotels when sometimes they were never given complete information from the CVB in the first place.

  We know part of your value to hotels is to serve as a liaison and aggregator of RFPs. Many CVBs pull the basic information from an RFP, place it into their own format, and distribute it to the appropriate properties. Please attach our complete RFP (minus our contact information if requested). Your hotel partners look foolish when they contact us for information that was in the original RFP. We blame them for not reading it, when maybe they were never given it in the first place (believe me, we know CVBs are not always to blame).

- Shotguns are for hunting, not for RFPs. If we have a program that is only viable for three of your venues, please don't shotgun it out to every single hotel, motel and B&B in your membership. We know some of you are obligated to do so because of your by-laws or what-not. We strongly urge you to fight this policy! You are bleeding opportunities, because you are leaving really annoyed planners in your wake who won't be back, and furthermore, will tell their colleagues. They won't use you again if the result is a time-drain—your strongest appeal is time savings.

- If we request only to be contacted by you, it's really frustrating to be contacted directly by dozens of your suppliers. If we wanted to deal with them directly, we wouldn't have gone through a CVB.

  We know that the Internet makes finding us and contacting us easier than ever, so most of the time it's out of your control. But please do whatever you can to prevent this from happening. This includes sending along the original RFP as mentioned above, which hopefully precludes the need for them to contact us for more information. If they choose to contact the planners anyway, I hope it's through LinkedIn in a non-salesy way to build a relationship.

Planner Pet Peeves

- I really hope this next one was an isolated incident. One CVB in a major southern city was angry with a planner who did not use them for her property search. When she contacted them for comp city maps and brochures, they declined and offered to charge her…to promote their city to her out-of-town visitors! I know that sometimes planners are guilty of going around you. They start out working with you, and then end up booking directly with a property. This is unethical and I hope my colleagues realize you need to be accountable for lead generation just like hotels do. I hope that the situation with the southern CVB was simply a misunderstanding.

CVB Proposal Quick Tip

Visit the RFP section earlier in the book for the three must-ask questions when you receive an RFP from us. Sending along our responses to these three questions will enable your hotel partners to really prepare a strong proposal.

FAMs

Familiarization trips can be a great marketing resource for destinations, if done well. Planners strongly believe that nothing beats face-to-face, and the same is true for destinations: nothing beats seeing them first-hand.

With the advent of social media, planners tell more colleagues than ever before about their destination experiences, for better or worse. The SPIN discussion board on LinkedIn is constantly humming with requests for destination suggestions.

While first-hand destination knowledge is best, it's harder than ever to get planners out of the office for a multi-night trip. These days, we have a difficult time justifying the time away, both to ourselves and to our clients or bosses. If it is a tropical destination, we have two added challenges: our co-workers can get really resentful, thinking that we're off sunning ourselves; and our bosses think we're off on a mini-vacation. They don't realize that most FAMs are exhausting!

Following are some tips if you are planning a FAM trip.

Planner Pet Peeves

- Most senior-level planners have overwhelmingly agreed that an educational component is critical to justifying the trip, both to themselves and their higher-ups. If CEUs (Continuing Education Units) are offered toward a designation, even better.

- We know it's important to maximize the short amount of time that you have us in your destination, but especially with the senior-level crowd, a daily hour-long break is appreciated so we can take care of business back at the office. If it's during business hours, even better, rather than at the end of the day.

- In 20 years, I've only been asked once this key pre-FAM question: what are my goals and objectives for joining the FAM? This is really helpful to structure your FAM activities to exactly what we want to experience in order to sell us on your destination. Isn't that better than a cookie-cutter FAM that's the same year-after-year?

Section IV: Non-Hotel Suppliers

- You will get better attendance if you market your FAM to a specific planner type, so we know our peers will be there. If you create a strictly senior-level FAM, like attracts like, and we'll be more likely to attend since there's a common thread and opportunities to network with colleagues. You also could offer a strictly government planner FAM, strictly pharma, strictly association planners, etc. It's much easier to plan targeted education this way as well, creating a really attractive FAM experience that's harder for us to pass up.

Planner Pet Peeves

Section IV: Non-Hotel Suppliers

CHAPTER 18.

DMCs

Personally speaking, I've had great experiences working with Destination Management Companies all over the world. They are a great asset to a planner needing to showcase a destination, find local resources, or enlist local expertise. I haven't heard any pet peeves that aren't isolated to a particular company. So rather than list some random gripes that apply to just a few, here are some tips from planners to help the rest.

Planner Pet Peeves

When a planner brings an event to a new city, she probably doesn't know any of the DMCs. She might ask her colleagues for recommendations, or search the Internet, so your reputation and your web site are critically important.

- Here's an idea to showcase your capabilities and your reputation. Get endorsements from planner clients right on your web site. Written endorsements are good, but video is great. If you can catch the planner at the actual event, fantastic. Bring along a camera with video capabilities, or your smart phone will do the trick as well.

  You're not going for high production value; you're trying to capture the emotion of the moment – like right after the big off-site gala that you helped to create. If you can catch the planner in that moment when she's experiencing that post-event euphoria, you're likely to get a fantastic endorsement. We planners can relate to that feeling, so the video will resonate with us. Upload it to YouTube and grab the code YouTube provides to put a little YouTube video box right on your web site. The more, the better.

- In the proposal stage, DMCs really need to stand out to win the business, especially if there's no prior relationship. Every DMC sends a nice proposal with beautiful photos and usually the same area activities that can be arranged. They all claim to have the best team and the best service. If the proposals are generally equal in the eyes of planners, that leaves you competing strictly on price, and you'd rather not do that.

  So how do you stand out to us? Get into our heads and think how we think. Before you send the proposal, ask us the three important questions: 1) what are our goals and objectives for the event, 2) what are the group's demographics, and 3) what are our top three priorities that we consider when making a decision. Then, be sure to mirror our responses at the beginning of your proposal, i.e. "I understand your goals and objectives for this event are..."

Nobody else does this, so you are sure to stand out.

Corporate Social Responsibility

CSR is huge right now for planners. As big as 'going green' was five years ago – that is how important CSR is in our industry right now. If we combine a charitable act in our meeting or event, it not only serves a community, but instills pride in our attendees. There are, of course, the business benefits of the goodwill PR opportunities, plus CSR helps in deflecting public opinion about a lavish incentive by focusing on the positive impact of the event.

It's a bit surprising that so many DMCs do not include CSR opportunities in their proposals. Along with the jungle tour and the zip line, why not offer opportunities to arrange opportunities to paint local schools, plant a garden or build a small library?

I experienced a great CSR activity at the SITE SoCal holiday event a couple years ago. We were split into teams and had to recreate world monuments with canned foods. The cans were then donated to a local food shelter. I believe such an event would resonate more

Section IV: Non-Hotel Suppliers

with planners as a team-building activity more than the usual, tired beach Olympics. If your DMC offers to coordinate this, you not only help your local community, you look really creative in the planner's eyes, and we don't mind paying you what we would have paid for other team-building activities.

Also, you could arrange opportunities for planners to buy room drop gifts from local handcrafters in need rather than big commercial operations (hint: we will pay more if it supports the needy). Photos of the charities that would be helped are a fantastic addition to your proposal.

Lastly, there is a great charity out there called Clean the World (www.cleantheworld.org). They collect leftover soaps and shampoos from hotel rooms, sanitize everything, and send them to needy parts of the world to save lives. It saves these items from landfills and recycles them to help others. A DMC could offer this as part of a proposal as well.

In closing, if you create an entire CSR section in your proposals or on your web site, you'll really be aligned with our own goals and objectives as CSR becomes a key component to most meetings and events.

Planner Pet Peeves

CHAPTER 19.

Convention Centers

The biggest complaint among planners is that the shows at convention centers incur costs that are spiraling way out of control.

"I have planned very large conferences, the largest being over 70,000 International delegates," said Dana Rhoden, CMP, CMM, Principal, the Veterinary Education Network in Dallas. Conferences that large, anything over 20,000 delegates, will restrict you to a few cities and you have to rotate to the same few cities. The cities as well as the convention centers, hotels and decorators all know you are limited in choices and take advantage of your restrictions. In many cases they simply refuse to work with you and continue to charge increased pricing, passing many costs to your exhibitors, who are in turn unhappy. When you present new ideas you often get push back as it appears they want the status quo."

The McCormick Place Case Study

McCormick Place in Chicago drew national attention a couple years ago because union labor policies had made the convention center very uncompetitive, and major shows were relocating to less expensive cities. Fortunately for the city of Chicago, they have made real progress toward lowering costs to bring business back.

With an end to the recent litigation between unions and the city, McCormick Place "now can put in place an 'exhibitors' bill of rights' that lets show managers and exhibitors set up their own booths with simple tools. Exhibitors also can drive and unload their own vehicles at McCormick Place, and union work can be done by two-person crews instead of the old minimum of three," according to an October

Section IV: Non-Hotel Suppliers

2011 article by David Roeder, Business Reporter for the Chicago Sun-Times.

The union situation is a major issue with many convention centers, and McCormick Place hopefully will now pull business away from the centers that have let costs get out of control. Chicago Mayor Rahm Emanuel said it best (in the same Sun-Times article): "This is the worst news for Orlando and Las Vegas: McCormick Place is open for business."

I believe that planners brought about this sweeping change in Chicago: they pulled their conventions and threatened never to return unless the center and the unions lowered costs and cut through all the horrible red tape they experienced to put on a show there. This lost business, along with the press catching wind of it, was what made Chicago take action.

I heard a few years back that one notoriously union-heavy city actually added a Podium Union in the 2000s. A *Podium Union*. (NOTE: inside joke for all you CMPs out there: we know 'lectern' is the correct terminology! If they are going to charge us to move one, they should know what it's really called.) I really hope that doesn't catch on.

It's bad enough when we have to have shadow labor when we bring in our own production companies. It's ridiculous that we have to pay a union electrician to plug in a computer or a union laborer to carry a box across the show floor. These practices are driving business away and encouraging planners to find alternatives.

We know that major changes to union policies are beyond the scope of our supplier partners alone. We simply hope that McCormick Place's sweeping changes put pressure on other major convention cities to enact change. I know we planners will continue to do our part to place business in cities that are more cost-effective and work like partners, not bankers. Lowering convention costs will result in *more* business for the city and *more* work for union members in the end, if they're willing to release their strangle-hold on their employers.

The Deal with Decorators

The exorbitant costs of doing business at convention centers don't fall just on the company hosting the show; they hit exhibitors the worst, in many cases. Major decorators have exclusive deals with convention hosts. One-stop shopping for everything certainly makes the planner's job a lot easier, but it creates a monopoly situation where the decorator can charge whatever they want, because they're exclusive. When an exhibitor has to pay $700 to have their carpet vacuumed (which they already paid thousands to have installed), something is just not right. It doesn't end there – exorbitant shipping and labor costs make it prohibitive for many exhibitors to participate in the show, which means lost revenue for the planner's budget.

Is this the show decorator's fault? No. It's just doing what the market will bear, and planners haven't been vocal enough about it to bring about change.

"I encourage planners to continually compare costs as sometimes it is easy to get complacent," said Rhoden. "You assume you are getting fair pricing when in some cases you are not. Just because you are a large show doesn't mean you are getting the best pricing."

In Summary

These comments are from a senior-level planner with a large foodservice show in Chicago:

Planner Pet Peeves

"Simply put, the biggest pet peeve is their unwillingness to share information until you are 'crossing a bridge' OR the bill comes due. I recently asked for some info about room charges at the convention center for the 8th time.

"Part of it," says the planner, "is that the center (decorator, AV vendor, etc.) knows that it might be shared with other shows (which might have other pricing) and they may have to [match] it.

"Case in point, in 2011, we challenged [a convention center] about electricity charges in the meeting rooms indicating that it was included while the center contended it was not. I researched and found 2 references, one (1) in a document sent to our office as well as one (1) online reference. The center relented but as soon as their reorganization was completed this past fall, they sent updated information noting that power does not come with a meeting room (how absurd).

"I find this practice abhorrent since it basically nullifies previous planning and affects budgets; it would not likely materially alter plans but it might shift some thinking in order to allocate for these 'hidden' fees."

Section IV: Non-Hotel Suppliers

CHAPTER 20.

Transportation Companies

Planners generally view transportation companies as a commodity. There usually isn't a lot of distinction between companies based on how they market themselves. They all generally claim to have updated fleets and great service.

These days, what can set you apart is safety. With the series of bus accidents that have befallen tour groups lately, planners are concerned. Drivers who are poorly trained, overworked, or not properly background-checked are the big issue. More than ever

Planner Pet Peeves

before in our industry, planners are focused on risk management and transportation is under that umbrella of concern.

"My biggest questions for transportation companies: 1) are their drivers employees, and 2) does the company own its own equipment? I need to know where the liability is," said Sharon L. Schenk, CMP, Founder, Your Meeting Professional in Connecticut. "I want to get a certificate of insurance, make sure background checks are done on drivers. I prefer not to deal with a middle-man; I want to deal with the company that actually owns the equipment."

If you're a transportation company, you can differentiate yourself by directly addressing the issues above on your website. We expect you to say you have great service and a nice fleet; we don't expect you to candidly tell us how you address our biggest safety concerns. Tell us how you background-check your drivers, and that you have a zero-tolerance policy for driver issues, and you'll earn our confidence.

SECTION V.

Starting Now

> "Everybody has accepted by now that change is unavoidable. But that still implies that change is like death and taxes. It should be postponed as long as possible and no change would be vastly preferable. But in a period of upheaval, such as the one we are living in, change is the norm."
> --Peter F. Drucker

Planner Pet Peeves

Section V: Starting Now

Thanks for Sticking With Me...

I know what I've said in this book has been one-sided, often maddening, and downright brutal. Hopefully it's been helpful and enlightening, too. I know we planners are flawed and very demanding. But we're also loyal – if you can get into that inner circle, we'll be incredibly devoted customers, and many of us will even become brand ambassadors who will tout your company to our peers when you really impress us. I see it happening all the time among my colleagues.

My goal for this book was to expose all the secrets that planners never share, so that change can happen. I had a tremendous amount of help from planners who openly shared their issues and allowed me to quote them, despite any potential backlash. This tells me that change is happening already – not a single colleague who was asked to participate said "no" - they didn't hesitate to share what they perhaps have never told suppliers before, for the greater good of the industry.

I know you have many, many pet peeves about planners. I've been collecting these from suppliers all over North America for another book. Believe me, suppliers are just as secretive about their pet peeves as planners are.

I hereby commit to writing a book called Supplier Pet Peeves to give you equal time. Planners need to hear what we do that drives you crazy, too. Then the industry will truly have changed. Will suppliers be as forthcoming in sharing their opinions on the record? Only time will tell. Certainly there's a bit more risk for suppliers to complain about their customers.

Starting Now

As I said before, I believe nothing changes without planners actually sharing what we *really* think. We have done a terrible job of that in the past. I'd say 'don't shoot the messenger,' but in this case, I'm a planner too, and guilty myself of doing many of the things in this book.

Now that I've been hearing all your supplier pet peeves across the country, I understand your frustrations with us.

Starting now, I aim to be a voice of change among my peers and my industry. Care to join me?

Planner Pet Peeves

Acknowledgements

I want to thank my wonderful authors' club members, Tracey B. Smith and Mike Vennerstrom for their honest feedback, support and encouragement – without whom I never would have met a single deadline; Tracey B. Smith and Sara Vanderbilt for always having my back and keeping me grounded while chasing shiny objects with me; Colleen Abernethy, Derek Wallace, Mike Dominguez, Julie Giorgio & Margie Sitton for understanding and supporting the mission of this book; my in-laws Mike & Karlin and friends Wendi Moore-Buysse and Paula Reel for cheering me on; Sarah Sladek and Larissa Schultz for giving me the confidence to follow in your footsteps; all my fantastic colleagues who openly shared their opinions and allowed me to quote them; MIL, Tracey and Kate for your editing and honest feedback; my parents for always being proud of me no matter what; and most of all, my wonderful, patient, supportive husband Greg, and my two brilliant, funny, inspiring kids, Annie and Will.

About the Author

Shawna Suckow, CMP, has been planning meetings and events since 1992. In 2008, she founded SPIN, the Senior Planners Industry Network, which is now the world's largest association comprised strictly of senior-level planners. Shawna consults with CVBs and suppliers all over the world to help them reach planners in the most effective ways possible, based on feedback from planners themselves. She speaks on several industry issues and has written for many industry publications. Shawna has been called extremely impatient and impulsive. Her favorite questions are "Why not?" and "What are you waiting for?" She is a master suitcase packer who, when not on the road, lives in Minnesota with her husband, Greg, kids, Annie and Will, and dogs, Alice and Henry. This is her first book.

Made in the USA
Lexington, KY
15 October 2012